FIRE EATING

A MANUAL OF INSTRUCTION

BY
BENJAMIN "GARTH" MACK

ILLUSTRATIONS BY
BRANDON MCKINNEY

BRIAN DUBÉ, INC.
NEW YORK

Published in the United States by Brian Dubé, Inc.
Manufactured in the United States of America

Library of Congress Cataloging-in-Publication Data
Mack, Benjamin, 1968-
    Fire eating : a manual of instruction/By Benjamin "Garth" Mack;
    illustrations by Brandon McKinney.--Rev. ed.
        p. cm.
      ISBN 0-917643-12-7
      1. Fire-eating--Handbooks, manuals, etc. I. Title.

    GV1559 .M24 2000
    793.8--dc21

                                                00-031455

First Printing, September 1993
Second Printing, February 1997
Revised Edition, First Printing, May 2000
Revised Edition, Second Printing, February 2002
Revised Edition, Third Printing, February 2003
Revised Edition, Fourth Printing, September 2004

CONTENTS

These page numbers are printed as a reference tool.
Do not try stunts out of order. Experience gained in the
earlier pages is critical for more complicated stunts.

FOREWORD TO THE REVISED EDITION

The original title of this manual was *HOW TO EAT FIRE WITH LITTLE OR NO PAIN*. At that time, the publisher did not want to include the word pain in the title and the title was changed. I myself no longer consider the previous title to be funny. It is abundantly clear that fire eating is too dangerous to be considered appropriate for anybody to attempt or perform. For that reason the publisher and I sincerely considered not reprinting this manual. However, as with many things that are dangerous, people will try them. With this in mind, our mission now is to present the safest methodology, to the best of our knowledge. This new revised edition has entirely new fuel, safety, and torch sections along with many other changes. The torch materials and wrapping technique recommended here are far safer than those in the previous edition. The previous fuel section has been discarded and replaced with updated material. Please keep in mind that although the information in this revised edition is current, fire eating is still very dangerous. In our attempt to make fire eating a little safer we would like to thank Eric Bagai for his contributions to the new Fuel and Safety sections.

Benjamin "Garth" Mack
May 2000

PREFACE

I learned how to eat fire for money. I swindled my way into getting booked on Milt Larsen's variety show *Hat$ Off* before I ever extinguished a flame. I performed for the run of the show, and while I was competent for opening night, it wasn't until I had a second degree burn that I became a good fire eater. I had learned all the fancy transfers quickly and thought I was invulnerable. Before the burn I was cocky; afterwards I was confident.

It is easy to learn the basics. It is easy to become over-confident with your new found talent. Please don't. I discourage you from trying these stunts because of the danger. Fire eating looks impressive, but it's not glamorous. The fumes stink, the fuel is bad for your liver, and it hurts to get burnt. Sideshow fire eaters are not choosing their profession because they love their work. They do it because it's a way to make money.

When I decided to eat fire, I found outdated books that recommended using asbestos. This is bad. Some of what I've written may become outdated, but it is currently the most up-to-date source on the market. Many amateur performers are going to use this book, and I hope I have saved them from a burn or two and have met your expectations. May I make an unsolicited suggestion: **Try sword swallowing. The swords taste better and you don't have to worry about the wind.**

INTRODUCTION

Apologies in advance for any statements that appear too basic or obvious. At the risk of being patronizing, we state the bare basics to help prevent accidents stemming from ignorance.

Realize that the flame on your torch is hot. Fire eating is performed with real fire, and you must treat fire with utmost respect. This manuscript cannot teach you the respect necessary to handle the flames safely, but it can explain some things you should not do.

While the flame itself radiates heat, the majority of the heat rises. Skin exposed to the top of the flame burns more quickly than at the bottom of the flame. Performing outdoors is extremely dangerous since a slight wind can push the tip of the flame back onto the skin and burn you.

WARNING

Fire eating is entertaining because performers appear to defy the laws of nature. They do not, but they push these laws close to the limit.

Do not take our warnings lightly. This manuscript is an inappropriate gift for a small child. It also is inappropriate for an enthusiastic adolescent or teenage performer. Instead, it is a concise, comprehensive guide for adults to the basics of fire eating.

Each stunt described is potentially dangerous. You should practice each stunt several times with an unlit torch until you know exactly what the stunt entails and are confident that you can properly perform it. To paraphrase the writer James Allen, "Whether you think you can or you think you cannot, you are right."

REALIZE THAT FIRE EATING IS EXTREMELY DANGEROUS AND THAT THE READER UNDERTAKES ANY OF THESE STUNTS ENTIRELY AT HIS/HER OWN RISK. THE AUTHORS AND ANY PUBLISHERS, DISTRIBUTORS AND DEALERS INVOLVED IN PRODUCING AND SELLING THIS MANUSCRIPT WILL NOT BE HELD LIABLE FOR ANY ACCIDENTS OR MISHAPS.

REMEMBER: *the reader tries and performs any of these stunts completely at his/her own risk.* The authors and anyone else commercially involved in producing and selling this manuscript will not be held liable. If the reader has any doubts about attempting any of these stunts, follow the prudent and reasonable approach and do not try it.

Important Terms

There are two basic types of fire manipulation: retention and extinguishment. All the stunts described are variations of these two principles.

Extinguishing is the act of putting out the flame using one's body.

Retention is the act of maintaining a flame separate from the torch.

1 SAFETY

A Few Safety Rules:

1) **NEVER INHALE.** Internal burns constitute the most serious injury sustainable from fire eating. Many stunts require exhaling, but you should never catch your breath with the flame in your mouth. Inhale before placing fire near your mouth.

2) **Never perform intoxicated.** It takes only one mistake to burn yourself or others. The margin of error can be slim. Don't be foolish; take no chance.

3) **Avoid performing outdoors.** If you must, allow the wind to blow from your side. This adjustment will prevent a small gust from blowing over your chin or into your nose and over your eyes.

4) **Practice.** Always practice the stunt first with an unlit torch. Read the instructions several times visualizing the stunt in your mind. Remember, these are not card tricks; you do not want to have a real run through the first time. For blasts, practice with water. Do not use real fuel until you can produce a fine, even spray with water.

5) **Watch out for hair.** Never try stunts on hairy parts of your body. Fire on the back of the hand will singe the hair and burn the hand. Furthermore, many mustaches preclude fire-in-mouth stunts. Proceed with caution.

6) **Clothing.** Do not wear clothing made from synthetic fibers. Use natural fibers such as cotton. Synthetic fibers will catch fire quickly and melt into burning flesh.

7) **Do not keep a lighter in your pocket after lighting up.**
It can explode if your clothing should catch fire.

Basic Safety Equipment:

Metal or plastic fuel containers. Do not use glass! We recommend fluorinated PE or PP Nalgene® fuel containers (*see chapter on fuels for more on containers*)

Airtight metal storage container for torch(es). A cylindrical metal food storage container will work nicely.

A large 100% cotton towel to smother flames should your hair or clothes catch on fire.

A small towel for wipe-ups of fuel on yourself or anything else. Keep this towel separate from your large towel.

A small fire extinguisher.

Someone standing by to help in the event of an emergency. They should know how to use the towel and fire extinguisher.

How to Avoid Burns

Never inhale. (Does this statement sound familiar?) Always remain calm. If you feel a burn approaching, extinguish the flame. With mouth stunts, exhale any air remaining in your lungs. While practicing, it is a good habit to keep a damp rag nearby to help immediately extinguish any small fires on your hand or anywhere else.

If your mouth is dry, discontinue practicing. Your saliva is your best protection from the flame. Likewise, if your hand becomes pink, tender, or sore, discontinue practicing. The oils from your palm also protect you from burning.

Be aware of lip ointments that might be flammable.

Before performing any stunt, shake excess fuel out of the torch.

Be aware that when the torch is turned upside down, the flames may touch your hand.

Incidentally, if you are performing indoors, especially in someone's home, you may want to appear to be extra cautious by bringing a small fire extinguisher with you. The theatrical benefits are not insignificant, you will gain peace of mind if you are nervous, and you are ready to mitigate any damage that might occur in case the improbable happens and you start a fire. We have never needed to use one, but they are inexpensive, take up little space, and are tax deductible if your performances constitute a business as opposed to a hobby. If you have any additional questions about this last point, consult your friendly, neighborhood tax preparer.

Finally, when performing indoors, realize that smoke from your torches may discolor the ceiling depending on the paint used and your torch and fuel. The lower the ceiling, the more concentrated the smoke will be and the greater the chance of damage. That's right, yet another risk to consider in performing these effects.

2 FUELS

Fuels Used For Fire Eating

Many fuels have been used for fire eating. All are toxic and have health risks, some more than others. Since the last edition of this book, there has been much more dialogue and research regarding health and safety risks with all the various fuels which have been used for fire eating. Any individual who is considering fire eating should: a) Familiarize themselves with all the various fuels and their hazards; b) Read the ingredients of any fuel to be used — many petroleum based fuels are a mix of 2 or more compounds. If possible obtain an MSDS (material safety data sheet) from the retailer or manufacturer. The MSDS will list the ingredients by percentage and the known health risks of the product.

We make no recommendations as to fuels since we do not believe that fire eating can be done with acceptable risk. Aspiration of even a small amount of fuel can cause chemical pneumonitis and pulmonary edema/hemorrhage. The following is a list of fuels which have been used by Fire Eaters and is provided for information purposes only.

Liquid Fuels

Kerosene (Paraffin Oil in the U.K.)

Lamp or Candle Oil —Paraffin based oil.

Coleman Fuel — (White Gas) Naptha based with various additives.

Charcoal Lighter or **Starter Fluid** — Mix of naptha and kerosene.

Lighter Fluid — Ronsonol™ or Zippo™. Naptha based with various additives.

Gasoline, paint thinner

Benzene

Alcohols — Methanol (wood alcohol), isopropyl alcohol (rubbing alcohol), denatured alcohol, and ethanol —Methanol and isopropyl alcohol are poisonous. Denatured alcohol is used for industrial purposes and is ethyl alcohol mixed with denaturants to prevent use as a beverage, thereby rendering it poisonous. Ethanol (grain alcohol or drinking alcohol), high proof liquor and Everclear (100% pure) have been used. However, absorption while working with it will lead to intoxication.

DO NOT USE ANY FUEL CONTAINING LEAD!

Dry Fuels

Lycopodium Powder (Dragon's Breath and other brands)
Custard Powder
Cocoa Powder
These powders have been used successfully for blows/blasts and have the obvious advantage of being non-toxic. Powders generally need to be held in a carrier (a tube) in the mouth. Be careful not to inhale the powder!

Fuel Containers

Use metal or plastic fuel bottles. We recommend Nalgene® fluorinated polyethylene containers—either a wide-mouth container or one with a nozzle. Nalgene® labware is airtight and leakproof and has been used successfully for years as a portable fuel container. Regular polyethylene is slightly permeable; fuels will actually pass through the wall itself. Fluorinated containers are gas impermeable.

Do not use glass containers to hold fuel. They can break and disperse fuel. Even when closed they can explode if in contact with a flame for more than a few seconds.

Using Fuels

You can either pour the fuel onto the torches or dip the torches into the fuel. (*See Fuel Containers section above*).

Many stunts are considerably more difficult if adequate fuel is not on the torch, but you should always shake excess fuel off of the torch before beginning any stunt. Excess fuel can drip down the torch's handle and result in a flame on the handle that you cannot control: (a) there is a flame burning on the handle that can cause you to drop the torch; (b) trying to extinguish this flame in your hand or mouth is impossible because there will be areas of the torch that you cannot contain. Failing to extinguish the entire flame allows for the flame still burning to reignite the rest of the torch. Furthermore, if there is excess fuel and you try extinguishing the torch in your hand, the fuel will seep onto your hand and ignite, leaving you with a handful of fire.

3 TORCHES

Torches

Many styles of torches are used for fire eating and have typically been made by the fire eater. The following design is a typical construction.

Items used:

1) Steel rod - 0.125" (3 mm) diameter by 14" (35.5 cm) long. A threaded portion on one end is ideal to prevent the wick from falling off. A fully threaded rod is an acceptable second choice. You may need to purchase a 36" rod (threaded on each end or fully threaded) and cut it to proper length pieces.

2) Kevlar (Aramid fiber) wicking. Available from juggling equipment suppliers - preferably NON-wire inserted (wire will get very hot and result in possible burns). Either Kevlar yarn can be used or 2" wide flat woven wick. For each torch, approximately 40" of yarn is recommended; with flat woven wick approximately 9-12" is recommended. The yarn is preferred by most fire eaters — with it, the construction of a fire eating torch is somewhat simpler.

3) Kevlar thread. Optional, depending on the construction of the torch. If you use Kevlar yarn, you can "whip" it to the metal rod (see below), and no thread will be needed to secure it. Cotton thread is not recommended - it can burn and break.

Construction:

Cut the rod into 14" lengths (using a bolt cutter or hacksaw), making sure that each has a threaded end. Wrap or whip the wicking around the threaded tip of a rod and form a swab approximately 2" wide by 0.75" diameter. If you are not using the "whipped" construction for yarn, or are using flat woven wick, secure the yarn or wick with Kevlar thread.

Whipping Technique for Securing Yarn:

This technique is similar to that used to whip ends of rope to keep them from fraying.

Double back about 3″- 4″ of the yarn and lay it along the rod with the looped portion extended slightly past the end of the rod.

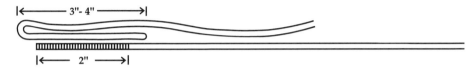

Wind the string tightly back and forth over approximately 2″ of the doubled part, leaving the looped portion and the short end of the yarn sticking out.

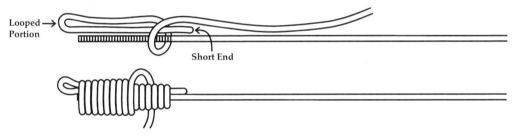

If you make three passes, you will finish with the end of the yarn near the looped portion of the torch. Tuck the end through the loop. Pull the short end (use pliers if necessary), drawing the loop and the long end under the binding.

Cut the short end flush with the binding. Voila!

4 FIRE ON HAND

Fire on Hand

Effect: Fire burns on the hands without the torch.

1) Place the torch lightly on the ball of the hand.

2) Remove it.

Note:

- If the fire begins to feel hot, close the hand or extinguish the fire any other way. In the beginning, be brief.

- Remember to keep the damp rag handy.

- A well soaked torch makes the stunt easier but too much fuel will linger on your palm and burn your hand. Repetition will burn off the hand's natural oils that protect you. If continued, your hands will become tender and red (this is not good). Continuing further could develop into a first or second degree burn.

Extinguishing a Torch in the Hand

Effect: The performer places a lit torch in the hand and extinguishes it.

1) Gingerly place the torch on the palm of the hand.

2) In one swift motion, close the hand around the flame and lightly squeeze. Pause. What you are doing is cutting off the oxygen from the torch so that it can no longer burn. Therefore, it is extremely important that your fingers remain close together and that you do not open your hand too soon.

3) Once you are positive the fire is out, open the hand.

Note:

- If you open your hand before the flame is extinguished, you will have fuel on your hand and an open flame. Remain calm and extinguish the flame swiftly with the damp rag. This stunt is one of the few that is easier to perform with a non-moist torch.

- The wicked portion of the torch should be pointing upward. Since fire rises, this positioning prevents the flame from escaping your grip around the little finger and thumb allowing you to suffocate the flame (*see diagrams below*).

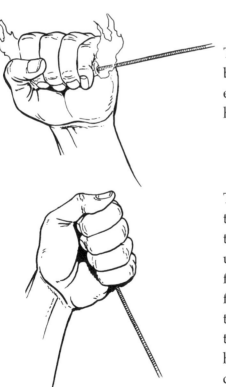

WRONG
The flames are exaggerated, but the torch cannot be extinguished when the flame has an oxygen source.

CORRECT
The thumb is over the top of the fingers, and the hand is tilted (remember fire burns upward) to prevent the fire from escaping by the little finger. Be careful to avoid touching the metal part of the torch. The metal will have heated up considerably and can burn your hand.

Flame Transfer

Effect: The performer places a lit torch on his hand, removes it, and lights an unlit torch from the hand.

1) Grip the two torches securely in a "V". One is lit, the other is unlit.

2) In one motion, press the lit torch to the hand, remove it, and ignite the unlit torch from the burning hand.

3) Close the palm to extinguish any residual flames.

Note:

- While each torch must be wet with fuel, the first torch must be very moist to perform the stunt with ease.

- Practice with unlit torches until this sequence becomes one fluid movement (*see diagrams below*).

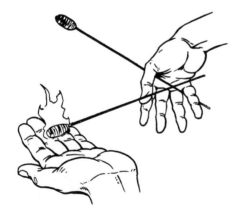

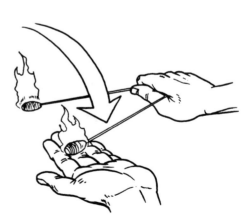

5 FIRE IN MOUTH

Fire in Mouth—Safety

Before discussing the following stunts, which are among the most spectacular in a fire eater's repertoire, please keep the following rules in mind. Not following them could result in significant injuries.

1) Only breathe out. This rule has been stated earlier.
   We repeat it to emphasize its importance.

2) Tilt your head back almost parallel to the floor.
   While this position might feel uncomfortable, it prevents you from burning the hairs in your nostrils.

3) Never let your lips touch the metal of the torch.
   Remember, it is the metal rod that can burn you instantly.

4) Most stunts should be performed with the wind to your side, thus blowing the flame away from the body, and not over the chin or mouth.

Note:

- Always have the wind behind you when performing the following stunts: **BLAST**, **POCKET BLAST**, and **BREATHING FIRE**.

- Please reread these rules and cautionary instructions.
  On the following pages, stunts in which fire is placed in the mouth are covered.

WARNING: Excess fuel around the mouth will ignite, so make sure you have no fuel on your face when placing the torch to your mouth.

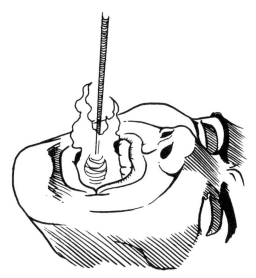

Placing Fire in Mouth

First, practice with an unlit torch.

1) Tilt your head back and lower an **unlit** torch in your mouth.

2) Remove the torch.

3) When you are ready to try this stunt for real, shake off any excess fuel before lighting the torches.

4) Lower the torch into your mouth and remove it <u>immediately</u>. If flame remains in the mouth, exhale.

Note:

- Be sure to lower the torch directly into the mouth. A diagonal approach not only risks burning your lips but is also a considerably more difficult flame to extinguish and manipulate.

Extinguishing Torch in the Mouth

Effect: The performer places the torch in his mouth and removes it extinguished.

1) Place the torch vertically in your mouth.

2) As you close your mouth, exhale slightly, thereby extinguishing the flame. The audience should not realize you are exhaling.

3) When you are positive the flame is extinguished, open your mouth and remove the torch.

Note:

- Keep your lips pulled away from the metal rod so you don't burn them. If necessary, touch your teeth to the rod to ensure that the flame is suffocated immediately.

- Remember that the act of exhaling should be imperceptible. The audience should think you are eating the flame, not blowing it out. The first few times you try the stunt, exhale very hard so the flame is extinguished faster. It is intimidating to have a flame in your mouth. Finesse will come with practice.

- If the flame reappears once you have removed the torch from your mouth, exhale with any remaining air in your lungs and close your mouth. This will extinguish the flame.

- Many performers stick out their tongue to guide the torch into their mouth. Some find this helpful, but be careful not to burn your tongue on the metal rod

- The torch need only go in your mouth far enough so that you can engulf the entire swab.

Fire on the Tongue

**Effect: The performer places a lit torch on his tongue.
When removed, the fire remains.**

1) Wet your tongue with saliva. **This stage is important; do not forget to do it each time you perform the stunt.**

2) Tilt your head back and extend your tongue.

3) Lightly press the lit torch on your tongue and remove it.

4) Exhale or close the mouth to extinguish the flame.

Note:

- The torch must be sufficiently moist to perform this stunt. Rolling the torch while lightly pressing down allows more excess fuel to remain on your tongue. Consequently, the flame will last longer.

- Remember that the rod will instantly burn your tongue, so do not touch the rod to your tongue.

Transfer from Tongue

Effect: Fire on tongue is used to light an unlit torch.

1) Hold one torch in each hand.

2) Maintain "Fire on Tongue."

3) As the lit torch is removed, touch the other torch to your tongue. Close your mouth to extinguish the flame *(see diagram below)*.

Note:

- Before trying this stunt with lit torches, practice so that the sequence is one fluid motion.

- Mastering the "Fire on Tongue" stunt is critical for this feat. Learning to sustain the flame on the tongue for longer lengths of time is helpful to this stunt and more impressive to the audience.

- Don't breathe during this stunt. **Breathing in is suicidal.** Exhaling will extinguish the flame.

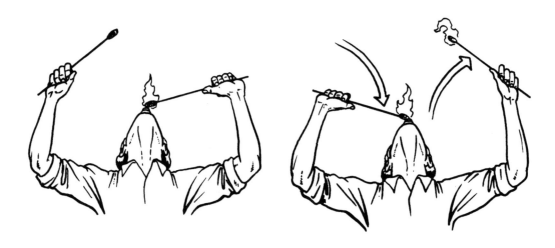

Teething

Effect: A lit torch is held between the teeth.

1) Tilt your head back and bring the torch vertically down.

2) Place the torch only part-way in your mouth.

3) Grip the torch with your teeth and exhale *(see diagram below)*.

4) Initially, hold the torch for a few seconds and then remove it.

Note:

- **Do not inhale.** Exhaling slightly will push the flame away from the lips and mouth.

- Smile! Smiling pulls your lips away from the flame.

- If performing outdoors, exhale harder to compensate for any wind that might be pushing the flame back over your mouth.

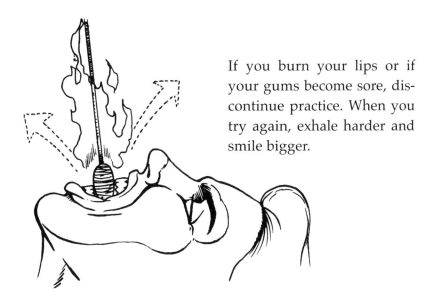

If you burn your lips or if your gums become sore, discontinue practice. When you try again, exhale harder and smile bigger.

Human Torch

Effect: A torch is placed in the mouth and removed.
Fire remains in the mouth.

1) Place the torch in your mouth and close it part way.

2) Pull your lips over your teeth, cupping the fumes in your mouth. Note that you do not want to be smiling but rather keeping your mouth in an "O" shape *(see diagram below).*

3) Watch, as the flame will diminish.

4) Keeping your mouth in the same shape, extract the torch.

5) Exhale or close your mouth to extinguish the flame.

Note:

- The flame will not remain if you remove the torch before the flame drops. The flame drops when the fire begins to burn off the fumes in your mouth.

- The way you hold open your mouth controls the size of the flame and its duration.

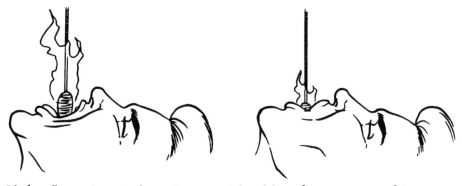

If the flame is not dropping considerably when you try this stunt, work on the shape of your mouth. The amount the flame drops also depends on the size of your torches. The larger the torch, the more dramatic the change in the size of the flame.

Human Torch Transfer

Effect: The performer lights an unlit torch from his burning mouth.

1) Hold one torch in each hand.

2) Maintain the "Human Torch."

3) Light the unlit torch.

Note:

- This stunt is easier with larger torches which are very moist. By closing your mouth as you exhale slightly, the flame will jump up. Thus by placing the second torch a few inches above your mouth, the flame can jump to ignite the second torch.

Two Torches in Mouth

Effect: Two torches are extinguished in the mouth at the same time.

1) Hold two torches as one.

2) Follow the directions for "Extinguishing Torch in Mouth."

Note:

- Be certain to exhale harder! The act of exhaling, however, should still be imperceptible to the audience. When first practicing, exhale as hard as you like. That is a big ball of fire in your mouth.

- The torches can be placed in your mouth from opposite sides, but that way is much harder.

- The flame is much larger with two torches than with one, and it is easier to burn your hand from the tip of the flame when the torch is inverted.

6 BLASTS

The Blast

Effect: The performer holds the lit torch vertically and propels a mass of fire three to five feet beyond the torch. This effect is perhaps the most spectacular stunt in a fire eater's repertoire but is also the most dangerous.

1) Place approximately half a shot glass of fuel in your mouth.

2) Hold the lit torch nine inches in front of your face.

3) Spray the fluid over the torch.

4) Step back and immediately wipe your mouth with a wet towel.

WARNING: Only perform this stunt if you can spray water in a very fine spray without any large globs or drops of water. The consistency is similar to an atomized mist as opposed to a spraying squirt. Furthermore, do not attempt this stunt if you are drooling any water after each try. A mistake in a performance could mean fuel on your face and, subsequently, catching on fire. A mistake could scar your face. **Do not attempt this stunt unless you are <u>completely</u> confident you can perform it properly.**

CORRECT

WRONG

The fuel needs to be atomized as it leaves your mouth.
If you are not sure it is atomized, it probably is not.
Practice with water.

Note:

- Always wipe your mouth immediately after blasting. This action removes any fuel on your face if you were sloppy. As you wipe your face, take a step back, thereby removing yourself from the flame. The blast, wipe, and step should be one continuous motion. The wipe and step happen concurrently after the blast.

- Any wind should be behind you so that it pushes the flame away from your body.

Pocket Blast

Effect: A small blast of fire extends over the torch. This blast is much safer than conventional fire eating and is a cute piece of comic relief.

1) Spray Binaca® (breath spray) in your mouth about fifteen times. **Do not inhale as you spray.**

2) Hold the torch approximately three inches away from your mouth.

3) Exhale over the flame.

Note:

- The danger in this effect is the flame igniting around your face. Do not exhale in a downward direction or too close to your face.

CREDIT: "Pocket Blast" was invented by **Rick Theis** of Hollywood, California and is published with his permission.

7 EXTRAS

Torch to Torch Transfer

Effect: Flame jumps from one torch to the other.

1) Start with two torches both soaked with fuel.

2) Light one of the two torches.

3) Hold the unlit torch horizontally at about eye level.

4) Hold the lit torch vertically about four inches below the unlit torch.

5) Raise and lower the bottom lit torch in a straight vertical motion. Properly executed, this movement will extinguish the lit torch while igniting the top unlit torch. This stunt is a little tricky to master but is very pretty. The flame does not actually jump but appears to do so because one torch is lit as the second is extinguished.

Note:

- This stunt in only possible with small torches because larger flames are impossible to extinguish with a simple vertical motion.

- Do not get discouraged. This stunt is difficult.

Breathing Fire

Effect: The performer places a torch in front of the mouth. By simply exhaling, a stream of fire extends beyond the torch.

1) Follow the directions for "The Human Torch," but close your mouth after the fire sinks.

2) Do not breathe until your torch is vertical in front of your mouth.

3) Exhale as if blowing a whistle.

Note:

- Closing your mouth on the "Human Torch" traps fumes in your mouth. These fumes ignite when exhaled over the open flame.

Balancing

Effect: The performer balances a lit torch on either his chin or nose.

1) Place a lit torch on your chin. Watch the top of the torch and compensate as it begins to sway.

Note:

- To learn the knack for this stunt, try practicing with a large, top heavy item such as a broom. Practice first with unlit torches and realize that a lit torch will act differently due to the flame's wind resistance.

- Leaning the item the minutest amount forward allows you to step underneath the item.

Balls of Fire

Effect: A ball of fire is placed in the mouth and extinguished.

The ball of fire is an ignited ball of cotton. The ball should be small, about one inch in diameter. This type of cotton ball is readily available as a cosmetic item.

1) Hold a lit torch in one hand. In the other hand, hold the cotton ball with your thumb, pinching it between your middle and index fingers.

2) Ignite the cotton ball on the torch. **Do not soak cotton balls in fuel.**

3) Drop the burning ball in the mouth. <u>Do not swallow the ball.</u>

4) Close your mouth, extinguishing the flame.

Note:

- Make sure you are using 100% cotton—not all cosmetic balls or "puffs" are 100% cotton. Even with cotton, the fumes are toxic by virtue of the carbon process from the smoke.

Lighting a Cigarette with Your Fingers

Effect: The performer touches the torch with his fingers and maintains the flame long enough to light a cigarette.

1) Press your fingers on the torch and maintain the fire.

2) Bring your lit fingers to the cigarette.

3) Inhale on the cigarette. (The surgeon general has proved that smoking is harmful to your health and causes cancer. Attempt this maneuver, as all the others in this manuscript, at your own risk.)

4) Wave your fingers to extinguish them.

Note:

- This entire action must be completed quickly. It helps to use larger torches for this stunt so as to have enough excess fuel on your fingers. Removing a little tobacco from the cigarette allows you to light the paper, which in turn lights the tobacco. Using unfiltered cigarettes allows you to inhale harder which will make the cigarette light faster.

Swallowing a Torch

Effect: The performer places a long torch in his mouth.
It appears as if he swallows it like a sword.

Build a torch using a telescoping antenna in place of the steel rod and the same wicking materials and construction techniques described in the chapter on torches.

1) Place the lit torch in the mouth.

2) Extinguish the flame.

3) Grip the torch with your teeth as you compact the antenna.

This effect might sound silly, but it looks impressive. Taking the collapsed torch out of your mouth and displaying it like a lollypop will produce a good response.

Afterword

DISCRETION

Fire eating is spectacular. For this reason it is highly commercial and can be a valuable selling point when booking shows. Because it is dangerous, however, the reader should consider the propriety of eating fire when children are present.

Naturally curious and imitative, children may well be tempted to try duplicating one of these dangerous feats for themselves. While they may not have access to torches, misfortunes could occur should a child try imitating one of these stunts on a smaller scale, perhaps with a candle, a cigarette lighter, or a match. Realize that not only could the child's actions harm him but they also could start a fire.

Given these possibilities of mishap, we caution against performing fire eating for audiences of primarily young children. For older children and adolescents, use your discretion and discuss it with the person who booked you. If you decide it is appropriate to perform the fire eating, be sure to preface the demonstration with an explicit warning to the children that they should not try to do what they are about to see, that only a trained professional should attempt this, etc. During performances, we have required all of the children present to raise their hands and solemnly promise not to try duplicating any of these stunts. Requiring an oath not only helps prevent mishaps but also impresses upon the audience the danger of what you are about to do. Thus there are substantial theatrical as well as safety benefits.

Do not overlook these considerations —they concern issues of both legal and moral responsibility.